TOOLS FOR CAREGIVERS

- **ATOS:** 0.5
- **GRL:** C
- **WORD COUNT:** 30

- **CURRICULUM CONNECTIONS:** animals, comparisons

Skills to Teach

- **HIGH-FREQUENCY WORDS:** at, be, can, have, let's, look, they
- **CONTENT WORDS:** animal, bare, big, ears, hair, short, small, tall
- **PUNCTUATION:** exclamation point, periods
- **WORD STUDY:** long /a/, spelled a (bare); long /a/, spelled ai (hair); long /e/, spelled ea (ears); long /o/, spelled o (short); /oo/, spelled oo (look); multisyllable word (animal)
- **TEXT TYPE:** information report

Before Reading Activities

- Read the title and give a simple statement of the main idea.
- Have students "walk" though the book and talk about what they see in the pictures.
- Introduce new vocabulary by having students predict the first letter and locate the word in the text.
- Discuss any unfamiliar concepts that are in the text.

After Reading Activities

This book compares opposite animal ears. Big and small, short and tall, hairy and bare. Pick one of the opposing pairs; for example: big and small. Make a list on the board with one heading that reads "big" and one that reads "small." Have the readers name animals with big and small ears, feet, bodies, legs, beaks, or tails. How many different animal parts can they compare?

Tadpole Books are published by Jump!, 5357 Penn Avenue South, Minneapolis, MN 55419, www.jumplibrary.com

Copyright ©2020 Jump. International copyright reserved in all countries. No part of this book may be reproduced in any form without written permission from the publisher.

Editor: Jenna Trnka **Designer:** Molly Ballanger

Photo Credits: Olhastock/Shutterstock, cover; nikpal/iStock, 1; StuPorts/iStock, 3; edurivero/iStock, 4–5, 2mr; Sonsedska Yuliia/Shutterstock, 6–7, 2br; Ann and Steve Toon/Alamy, 8–9, 2tr; Alina Wegher/Shutterstock, 10–11, 2bl; photomaster/Shutterstock, 12–13, 2ml; Anke van Wyk/Shutterstock, 14–15, 2tl; Daleen Loest/Shutterstock, 16.

Library of Congress Cataloging-in-Publication Data
Names: Gleisner, Jenna Lee, author.
Title: Ears / by Jenna Lee Gleisner.
Description: Tadpole edition. | Minneapolis, MN: Jump!, Inc., (2020) | Series: Animal part smarts | Audience: Age 3–6. | Includes index.
Identifiers: LCCN 2018042924 (print) | LCCN 2018043968 (ebook) | ISBN 9781641286923 (ebook) | ISBN 9781641286909 (hardcover : alk. paper)
ISBN 9781641286916 (paperback)
Subjects: LCSH: Ear—Juvenile literature.
Classification: LCC QL948 (ebook) | LCC QL948 .G54 2020 (print) | DDC 599.14/4—dc23
LC record available at https://lccn.loc.gov/2018042924

EARS

by Jenna Lee Gleisner

TABLE OF CONTENTS

Words to Know...........................2

Ears...................................3

Let's Review!.........................16

Index.................................16

pole

WORDS TO KNOW

bare

big

hair

short

small

tall

EARS

Let's look at animal ears!

ear

They can be short.

They can be tall.

They can be big.

ear

They can be small.

11

hair

They can have hair.

13

They can be bare.

LET'S REVIEW!

What are these animal ears like?

INDEX

bare 15

big 9

hair 13

short 5

small 11

tall 7